REACHING FOR THE STARS

TOM CRUISE
Movie Star

By Julie Bach

Published by Abdo & Daughters, 4940 Viking Drive Suite 622, Edina, Minnesota 55435.

Library bound edition distributed by Rockbottom Books, Pentagon Tower, P.O. Box 36036, Minneapolis, Minnesota 55435.

Cover photo: Black Star
Photo credits: Archive - pgs. 4, 10, 11, 13, 16
                Bettmann - pgs. 18, 20, 24, 25, 27, 29

Edited by Rosemary Wallner

LIBRARY OF CONGRESS CATALOGING-IN-PUBLICATION DATA
Bach, Julie S., 1963 -
    Tom Cruise / written by Julie Bach.
        p. cm. -- (Reaching for the Stars)
    ISBN 1-56239-228-X
    1. Cruise, Tom, 1962-   --Juvenile literature. 2. Motion picture actors and actresses -- United States -- Biography --Juvenile literature.   I. Title .
II. Series.
    PN2287.C685B3 1993
    791.43'028'092--dc20
    [B]   93-1981
                                                         CIP
                                                         AC

TABLE OF CONTENTS

A Taste for Adventure 5

A Lonely Childhood 6

Interest in Acting 8

An Early Break 9

Stardom 12

Challenging Roles 15

A New Romance 19

A Regular Guy 23

Caring About Others 26

Always a Winner 28

Tom Cruise's Address 31

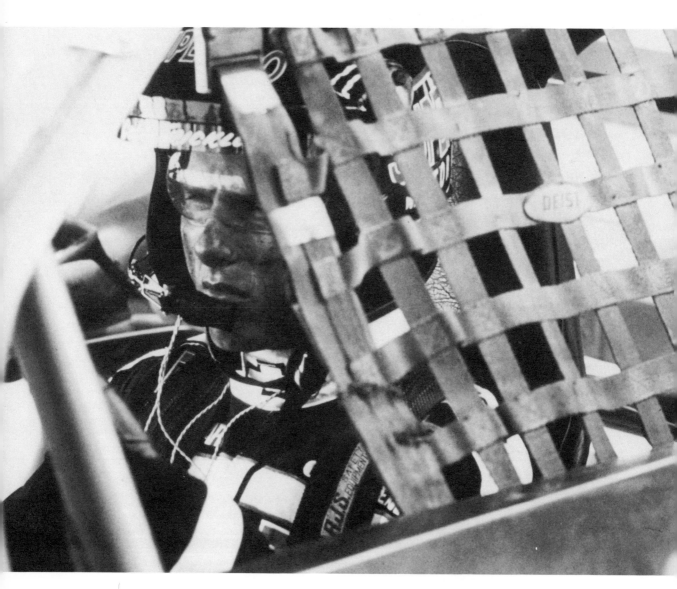

Movie actor Tom Cruise in the movie Days of Thunder.
Tom has a great love of race cars and spends a lot of time on the track.

A TASTE FOR ADVENTURE

The day is bright and warm in Daytona Beach, Florida. At the Daytona International Speedway, a single car races around the track. The car travels faster and faster. It goes so fast that it appears just on the edge of going out of control. Finally the car slows to a stop. A handsome young man jumps out of the driver's seat. "Yeah!" he yells to the handful of people who have been watching him. "I want to make a movie about this!"

The young man is Tom Cruise. He had driven the race car the way he does almost everything in his life—with energy and enthusiasm, and a desire to be number one. The appearance of danger is real. Tom takes risks all the time—in adventures like racing and skydiving and on the screen as an actor. His fearlessness and energy have made him one of the most successful actors in Hollywood.

A LONELY CHILDHOOD

Thomas Cruise Mapother IV was born in Syracuse, New York, on July 3, 1962. He was the only boy in a family with three daughters. Tom was close to his mother and sisters. When he was eight years old, his older sisters and their friends practiced kissing on him when they were beginning to date. "I grew up around women," he says. "I feel real comfortable around them."

Tom's father, an electrical engineer, had trouble keeping a job. He would start a job in one area, lose it, and then look for a job in a different area. Each time, Tom's father moved his family to a new home with new people. Before Tom was 12 years old, he and his family had moved twelve times. Each time, Tom's parents enrolled him in a new school. He found it hard to make friends. He was always the "new kid." The other kids already had their friends. Many times they did not accept him. "I never really seemed to fit in anywhere," Tom remembered.

When Tom was 12, his parents divorced. Sadly, Tom lost track of his father years after the divorce. His father died of cancer in 1984. He had never seen any of Tom's films. Tom and his sisters were raised by their mother, Mary Lee, a teacher. Money was tight; Mary Lee moved her children many times looking for better work. To help the family's finances, Tom attended a Catholic seminary during his freshman year of high school because he had won a scholarship. He never seriously considered becoming a priest, though. "Even at that age, I was too interested in ladies," he said.

In four years, Tom attended four different high schools. Besides always being the new kid, he found school hard because he has dyslexia. A person with dyslexia does not always read the words on a page in the right order. Today, most children with dyslexia get help in school. But when Tom was growing up in the 1960s and 1970s, not much help was available. He struggled on his own.

He did like sports, however. He tried out for many teams, including ice hockey, wrestling, and soccer. He was not an outstanding athlete, but he had energy. He was aggressive, driven, and not afraid to work hard. Coaches liked having him on their teams because he was so energetic.

INTEREST IN ACTING

During his senior year of high school, Tom could not try out for wrestling because he had injured his knee. He tried out for the school play instead. To his surprise, he landed the lead role. He found he was good at acting—and he liked it. He decided he wanted to become an actor.

When graduation day for Glen Ridge High School in New Jersey rolled around, Tom was nowhere to be seen. He had skipped his graduation so he could go to New York City. He was going to begin his acting career.

AN EARLY BREAK

Months after he arrived in New York, Tom got a break. He was given a small part in the 1981 movie *Endless Love*. Critics thought little of the movie, but they were impressed with this newcomer, Tom Cruise. Soon, he was given a part in the 1981 movie *Taps*. He played a fanatic military student. His role was small, but he performed so well that the director made the part bigger. The young man who had been so lonely as a child was on his way to success.

Tom's next film was *Losin' It*. The movie was a box office bomb, and not a very smart career move. Thankfully, critics and audiences forgot about it when Tom appeared next in *The Outsiders,* directed by Francis Ford Coppola, a well-respected director. The movie is about a group of street kids who have no parents and live on their own. Tom took his role as an outcast seriously. He skimped on showers for several weeks. He had a cap from his tooth removed. He wanted to look the part. Already in his short career, Tom was seeing the importance of hard work.

Tom Cruise plays Shawn, a military cadet whose fanatic attitude endangers his fellow cadets in the movie Taps.

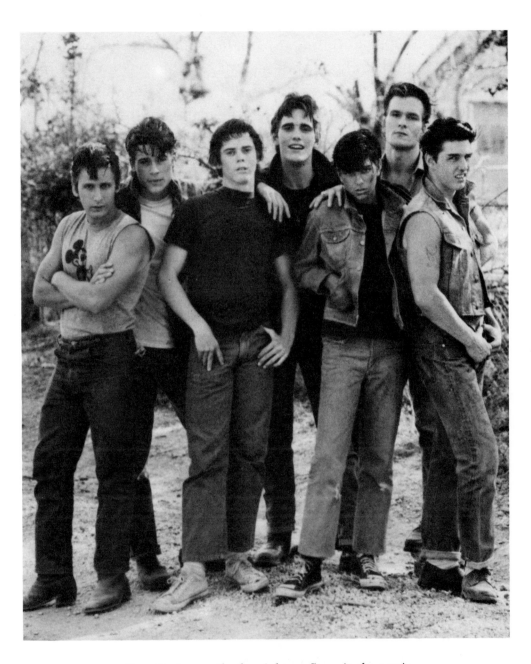

Tom Cruise, on the far right, as Steve in the movie
The Outsiders.

In 1983, Tom appeared in *Risky Business*, and his success was assured. He played the part of a teenager who has a wild time when his parents leave him home alone. Tom became a teen idol overnight. He also impressed the critics with his performance. Three short years after graduating from high school, the kid who had never fit in was a national celebrity.

STARDOM

How had this young actor managed to become a star in such a short time? People say it is his intensity. They say he is focused and driven. One producer who has worked with Tom said, "He commits himself to being the best he can possibly be." Tom says of himself, "Whatever I do, whatever I pick up, I get fascinated by it, and I want to understand it, and I get obsessed."

In 1986, Tom Cruise made two movies: *Top Gun*, with Kelly McGillis, and *The Color of Money*, with Paul Newman. He was starting to work with some of the best actors in Hollywood. Tom says he learned much about acting as he worked alongside Paul Newman. He considers the veteran actor a mentor. Making the movie was a learning experience for Tom. Newman was equally impressed with Tom Cruise. He began calling the young actor "Killer" because of his role in *Taps*.

Tom Cruise with Paul Newman in the movie
The Color of Money. *Tom considers Newman his mentor.*

The characters in *Top Gun* and *The Color of Money* are much like Tom himself—energetic and driven to be the best. They were characters that American audiences could admire. They were strong, decisive, and brave. And, of course, they were handsome. Many people are surprised to learn that brown-haired, blue-eyed Tom is only five feet, nine inches tall. But directors have never had to use film tricks or props to make Tom appear taller than he is. Somehow his presence on the screen is large enough in itself.

CHALLENGING ROLES

In 1986, Tom began dating Mimi Rogers, an actress. They were married in 1987. Tom was 23 years old. Mimi was 29 years old.

Tom's next two films appeared in 1988. The critics considered the first one, *Cocktail,* a silly movie. Even Tom admits it was not very good. But simply because he was the star, the movie did well in theaters. His other 1988 movie was a great success. Tom starred with Dustin Hoffman in *Rain Man.* It was the story of an autistic savant, a retarded man who is brilliant with numbers. Hoffman played the savant. Cruise played his brother. At first Tom's character dislikes his brother. Eventually, he comes to love him. Hoffman's performance earned him wide acclaim. But Tom Cruise's role was also critical to the film. He played his character with just the right touch so that audiences would feel what it was like to care for a person who is mentally disabled.

Tom's next role came in 1989. It would prove to be the most difficult of his career. Oliver Stone, the director, cast him in *Born On the Fourth of July.*

Tom Cruise with Dustin Hoffman in Rain Man.
This movie was a great success and propelled Cruise further into movie stardom.

Tom played the part of Ron Kovic, a real-life Vietnam veteran. Ron had been wounded in the war and was a paraplegic. That meant that his legs were paralyzed. He would never walk again. When he returned from Vietnam, he spoke out against the war. This made him unpopular with many Americans. Tom Cruise worked hard to prepare for his role as Ron Kovic. He spent days in a wheelchair. He learned how paraplegics get into bed from their chairs. He visited hospital wards where paraplegics were learning how to care for themselves. He wheeled around Los Angeles with Ron Kovic, learning about the man he would portray in the movie. Making the movie was physically and emotionally difficult. Kovic's life when he came back from Vietnam had been hard. As Tom played out his life, he felt all the pain. Tom relied on Mimi to help him get through the filming. "I wouldn't have been able to make it through *Born*, I don't think, without her being there," he said. "There were times I was so physically exhausted, and the stuff was very emotional."

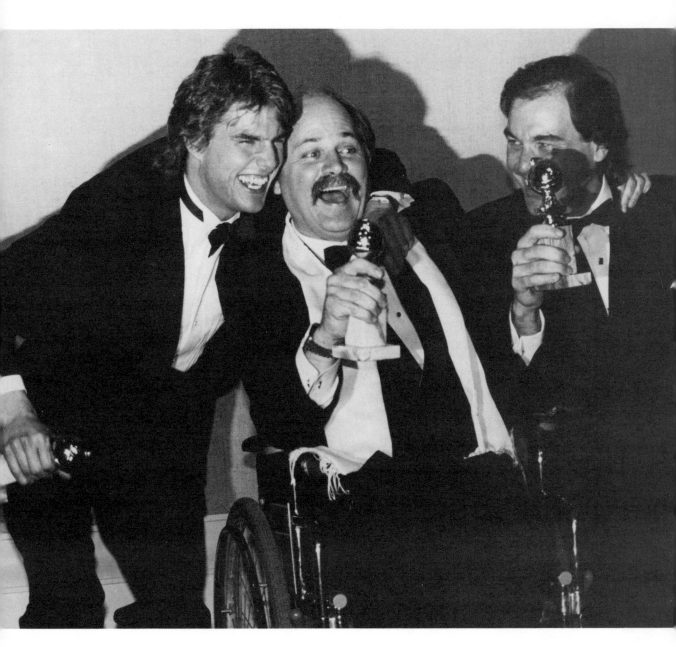

Tom Cruise with Ron Kovic, center, and Oliver Stone, right. Cruise played Kovic in the movie Born on the 4th of July. *Stone was the director.*

In spite of their support for each other, the marriage did not last. The couple separated in 1989. Tom never let on to the press that he and Mimi were unhappy. He wanted to protect their privacy. Their divorce was final in 1990.

A NEW ROMANCE

Tom Cruise did not stay single for long. In 1990, he filmed *Days of Thunder* with Nicole Kidman, an Australian actor. Their romance on screen became real off screen. The movie was about a young stock car driver. It had been Tom's idea. He had always liked racing. When he was a teenager, long before he got his license to drive, he and his sisters sneaked their mom's car out of the garage and drove around in the middle of the night. Tom really got interested in racing when Paul Newman introduced him to it. Newman owns several race cars and had invited Tom to drive one. Tom turned out to be a natural. After driving a car at the Daytona Speedway, he wanted to make a movie about racing. Several years later, he finally talked a studio into doing the movie.

Tom Cruise with his wife, Nicole Kidman.

In *Days of Thunder*, Tom played Cole Trickle, a brash and confident driver. Nicole Kidman played the part of a psychologist who helps Tom's character come to understand himself. And of course the two characters fall in love. But Tom's romance with Nicole did not start until the filming for *Days of Thunder* was nearly done.

The two actors kept their relationship as quiet as possible and out of the press. Then, on Christmas Eve 1990, they were married in Telluride, Colorado. Tom had rented a $2 million house with six bedrooms and a view of the Rocky Mountains. The morning of December 24, Nicole woke to find the house filled with flower arrangements. That evening, as the sun set over the mountains, Tom and Nicole were married. Their families and a few friends were present. Tom wore a black tuxedo. Nicole wore a white silk gown. The couple had written their own vows.

Tom and Nicole are both adventurous people. They like to skydive. Nicole, however, does not like car racing. The two have much in common and are happy that they got married. "Nic just makes me feel fun around her," explains Tom. "She makes me laugh."

Tom says Nicole helps him relax and enjoy life. He has always worked extremely hard at his career. "I work hard every day," he said, "and I expect that from everyone else around me."

Because Tom works so hard, directors find him easy to work with. On his next film, the 1992 hit *Far and Away*, Tom helped keep the production on schedule by setting an example of hard work for the rest of the cast. That also helped keep the film within budget. *Far and Away* is an old-fashioned romance about two people who travel from Ireland to America. Tom played a poor farmer who dreams of owning land in Oklahoma. Nicole was cast as a spoiled rich girl who fall's in love with Tom's character. Director Ron Howard says that Nicole and Tom's real-life romance added zest to the romance between their characters on screen.

After *Far and Away*, Tom began work on his next film, *A Few Good Men*. In this film, Tom played a young naval lawyer named Daniel Kaffee. Kaffee is chosen to defend two Marines accused of killing a third Marine. Jack Nicholson and Demi Moore also starred in the film.

The film had no action like the car races in *Days of Thunder* or the flight scenes in *Top Gun*. Instead, it had many courtroom speeches and long conversations. That meant Tom had to read and memorize more than usual. Tom's dyslexia makes him read slowly, but he knew how to work hard to overcome his reading problem. A producer for the film said, "We'd heard Cruise is not a great reader, and this film is nothing but words. But by the time we put film in the camera, he knew that character inside and out."

A REGULAR GUY

After more than a dozen successful movies, Tom Cruise is one of the most popular actors in America. In his early thirties, he is earning millions of dollars for every film he makes. His picture appears frequently on the covers of popular magazines. He is constantly in demand for interviews, though he gives just a few.

*Oscar night 1989, Dustin Hoffman gives Tom Cruise an
enthusiastic kiss after receiving their awards for the movie* Rain Man.

Tom Cruise waves to hundreds of fans as he receives his star on the Hollywood Walk of Fame.

Friends who know Tom say that he has not let fame affect him. He drives his own car, and does his own grocery shopping. He wears simple clothes like blue jeans and white T-shirts. His hair is cut in a simple style. Many Hollywood actors wear sunglasses to hide their identity from fans. Tom rarely does. Yet he never tries to draw attention to himself, either. Still, this famous actor causes a stir wherever he goes. Once, while filming *Days of Thunder* in Florida, Tom stepped into a department store. A friend entered the store just after Tom left. "The whole place was in an uproar," said the friend. "All the girls working there were out in the middle of the floor screaming."

CARING ABOUT OTHERS

Tom Cruise is described as a polite man with a genuine regard for others. He greets his elders as "Sir" and "Ma'am." In Daytona one day he spotted a man by the side of a highway. The man was holding a sign that said, "I'll work for food." Tom pulled over to the side of the road. He stepped out of the car and gave the man all the cash in his pocket, about $100.

Tom Cruise speaks to a large crowd during the opening ceremonies of Earth Day 1990 in Washington.

Then Tom shook the man's hand and said, "Take care." He's also generous to people who work with him. When the cast and crew of *Days of Thunder* held a New Year's Eve party, Tom bought all the refreshments. They cost thousands of dollars. He shook everybody's hand at the party and asked if they were having a good time.

Tom also is concerned about the environment. He recycles his trash. He conserves water by lowering the water pressure in his home. He also joined Earth Communications Office. The office is a group of celebrities who communicate environmental messages. "How can I ask other people to clean up the land, air, and water if I don't?" he asked.

ALWAYS A WINNER

Tom Cruise likes to live life on the edge. Racing cars is an example of his desire for speed and adventure. One friend recalled, "I have been in a car with Tom, and each time he was in the driver's seat, I was truly scared." But Tom is not just reckless. He is a natural at racing. He knows what he is doing.

Tom Cruise with wife Nicole Kidman at the Cannes Film Festival for the screening of their movie Far and Away.

One race team manager said, "Tom could easily have qualified in the top 20 for the Daytona 500." Tom brings this adventurous spirit and drive to his roles in movies. He is often cast as a champion, someone who triumphs over troubles: a fighter pilot *(Top Gun)*, a champion nine-ball player *(The Color of Money)*, a triumphant Vietnam veteran *(Born on the Fourth of July)*. Perhaps Tom can play winners because he himself is a winner. Despite his lonely childhood, his parents' separation, and his dyslexia, he has been successful.

Tom admires the experienced actors he has worked with like Dustin Hoffman and Paul Newman. But he is well on his way to becoming a great actor himself. And he's very happy with his life. "I never wanted to be someone else," he said.

TOM CRUISE'S ADDRESS

You can write to Tom Cruise at:

Tom Cruise
14755 Ventura Blvd., #1-710
Sherman Oaks, CA 91403